About the Basic Income FAQ

For friends, family, and other readers who may not have internet access, or perhaps don't know about Reddit, we have formatted this open source, community-developed FAQ from /r/BasicIncome with the deepest gratitude for all those who have worked together with us over the years on a volunteer basis, for the most part completely uncompensated, to improve the content of this document for the benefit of the community and ultimately, humanity.

Note to new readers: keep in mind that this is an internet resource, and as such, much of the wording is geared toward the assumption of embedded hyperlinks. This version of the document, based upon a snapshot taken in October 2018, contains 193 links to additional information – 187 endnotes, 6 inline references. In many respects, the links are perhaps the most valuable part of the document. In order to attempt to provide access to the same information for offline readers, we've extracted the links and provide them as endnotes. While the printable link list is nowhere near as useful as hyperlinks, we wanted to do our best to give as many people access to the full information available, as possible, in the open source spirit with which the FAQ was created, and continues to evolve.

For those who study the data for themselves and come to understand both the "what and why" of unconditional basic income (UBI), we have written a book outlining the how of transitioning the U.S. basic income movement from academic theory to formal, legislated policy. The November 2018 book is titled, Where We Go from Here: Chaos to Community | A Modest Proposal for the Livable Income Security Act of 2019. Library of Congress Control Number: 2018912670. Available in print (ISBN-13: 978-1732930001, ISBN-10: 1732930007, http://a.co/d/aocLjy2) and digital formats (ISBN-13: 978-1732930018, ASIN: B07K55PCX3, http://a.co/d/bLozX3w).

What is basic income?

"A basic income is an income unconditionally granted to all on an individual basis, without means test or work requirement."[1]

What are the benefits of basic income?

In no particular order:

Eliminates the "unemployment trap". Under current systems, when someone gets a job they lose most of their welfare payments. This means they can go from not working at all to working a full week without significantly increasing their income. This is a disincentive to work. Under basic income, when people got a job they would retain the same basic income payment, with their salary added to it, so the disincentive no longer exists.

Reduces government bureaucracy. A lot of government workers are required to ensure that welfare recipients are not claiming their benefits fraudulently, and to administer the complicated system of welfare payments and tax credits. The increased need for personal tax advisers also sucks skilled workers out of the productive sector. A basic income would hugely simplify the welfare system by replacing most of these bureaucracies, which would reduce its administrative cost significantly.

Clarifies the tax code. Taxes are way too complicated, and everything we can do to simplify them would be --all things equal-- a net gain in the value of human society. A basic income, coupled with a flat tax, is capable of mimicking all aspects of our current progressive (bracketed) taxation scheme, but without brackets. Everyone will, at the start of each year, know precisely what their taxes will look like; "predicting what tax bracket you'll be in" will no longer be necessary. All marginal tax rates will be identical, while the basic income ensures that net-taxes follow a progressive-tax structure. Also: a basic income, in the form of a "basic deduction", can replace and improve upon the "standard deduction" used by the IRS, which itself is problematic.

Exemplifies and emphasizes single-class policymaking. It is not structurally optimal to produce policies that explicitly divide people up into classes and then apply different laws to each class, as our bracketed tax code does (and as our welfare structure does). It is better to form a single law that applies to every individual: "Everyone gets $x in basic income, funded by a y% flat tax". When we are all in the same 'group', class divisions become less divisive, and we reinforce the principles of liberty and equality.

Greatly reduces fraud/waste/abuse. When welfare subsidies are contingent on conditions like employment, income level, number of hours worked, family status, etc., there are opportunities to game the system, either by illegally lying (fraud) or by simply obeying the economic incentives put in front of you (waste/abuse). These cause losses of real economic value, which are paid for by every taxpayer. Removing this incentive structure allows confidence in the welfare system's ability to reach people exactly as intended.

Guarantees a minimum living standard. Though it's subjective/politicized, people may be entitled to a certain basic standard of living, regardless of whether they are momentarily able to participate in the labor market. Universal Declaration of Human Rights, Article 25, states, "Everyone has the right to a standard of living adequate for the health and well-being of himself and of his family, including food, clothing, housing and medical care and necessary social services, and the right to security in the event of unemployment, sickness, disability, widowhood, old age or other lack of livelihood in circumstances beyond his control" (United Nations).[2]

Increases bargaining power for workers. Workers will be able to afford to refuse a job if the employer abuses its oligopoly or the workspace has poor conditions, so firms will be forced to improve the employment conditions and wages for their workers. This will happen as a natural result of negotiation between firms and workers, and will not require government intervention or unionization.

Lowers need for government regulations on the labor market. Policies such as the minimum wage will become less necessary with the basic income, as people will already get enough money to live on from the basic income. And negotiating power for workers will increase. This will allow the government to remove some of the regulations on the labor market, creating a freer market and providing benefits for both employers and employees.

Impacts immigration. With the minimum wage obsolete, manual labor can be priced at its fair-market value, meaning undocumented immigrants will have to accept even lower wages to compensate for their legal risks, potentially putting the standard of life lower than if they stay at where they were.

Reduces Gentrification. When only the residents of an area receive that area's Basic Income, housing and consumer goods prices are thus inflated, making it hard for other social groups to swoop in with a bunch of money and inadvertently pick apart the community. The BI gives a relative advantage to established residents, thus protecting the community structure.

Reduces the gender "pay gap." Women, on average, make less money than men, and debaters of this issue fall into two camps: (1) those who want to reduce that gap to help women achieve financial freedom, and (2) those who want to prevent the harmful effects of government pay-mandates and micromanagement. Basic Income is capable of satisfying both camps by giving all citizens a base income, making women (and people in general) less dependent on their work-income. And it does so without removing any of the beneficial capitalistic incentives to work and provide value. Furthermore, the gender pay gap is reduced for precisely those women who most need it: low-income women. It makes them less dependent on a potentially abusive spouse and less sensitive to pregnancy-based work issues, without unjustly interfering with the market's ability to set salaries for upper- and middle-class workers.

Improves mental health through income security. Mental health is one of the largest public health problems in most developed countries. The knowledge that the basic income will ensure a basic standard of living in any circumstances will provide a sense of mental security, especially when the economy is performing poorly. The removal of various dehumanizing tests and stigmatization of anyone who receives welfare payments will also serve to improve mental health. There is also evidence that poverty itself reduces cognitive capacity, comparable to a loss of 13 IQ points, or chronic alcoholism as compared to sobriety.[3] A basic income would remove this cognitive impairment.

Increases physical health. The rising cost of healthcare is a cause of great long-term concern, and basic income could lower this cost. In the Dauphin, Manitoba pilot experiment in Canada, an 8.5% reduction in hospitalization was found to be a direct result of the minimum income.[4] This was attributed to the reduction in workplace injuries and family violence resulting from the rise in incomes.

Stabilizes costs over time. Current welfare schemes have costs that fluctuate significantly with the performance of the economy, and are increasing as populations age and more people leave the workforce. The costs of basic income schemes would not see this fluctuation, as the basic income is paid to all adults regardless of whether they are in the labor force or not.

Simplifies implementation of progressive taxation. There's no need for "tax brackets" having different tax rates when people receive a basic income, since the BI effectively causes the same tax rate structure, only requiring two numbers to be chosen: the value of the BI allowance, and the flat tax rate. With less thresholds and tax rates to play around with, taxation becomes less politicized and less used as a weapon of class warfare. This also simplifies your IRS paperwork and

makes the tax structure smoother and thus non-susceptible to income-shifting.

Deals better with widespread unemployment. Some people argue that,[5] with the development of new automation technology and the increase in the labour force due to globalization, rates of unemployment in developed countries are likely to stay high and increase in coming years. This would impose a significant increased cost on current schemes, but as spending from the basic income would not increase, this system would be more able to cope with the change.

Recirculates money from capital to labor. Even if technology doesn't lead to high unemployment, it may well lead to lower wages and greater inequality. Capital - equipment and machinery that helps to produce things - is now creating a greater share of output compared to labour - human workers. This allows business owners, who own the capital, to pay workers the same or less while more is produced, so they make more profit for themselves. We are already seeing that output per worker is increasing,[6] while workers' wages are not. In the long term, this will mean that business owners make more and more money, while those who don't own capital will make less and less. Basic income alleviates this by taxing the rich (who will probably own capital) and giving money to the poor (who probably won't), even if they can't find a job.

reddit.com/r/BasicIncome/wiki/

Increases number of small businesses. Many people may currently be discouraged from leaving their job to start their own business, as if the venture fails they will have no source of income. The basic income would provide income to these people, so more people would feel able to start businesses, which could only increase innovation and competition in the economy. Evidence of this effect can be found in the Namibia basic income experiment, where those receiving it showed increased entrepreneurship with a 29% increase in average earned income, excluding the basic income.[7]

Increases charitable work and academic research. Much work in the charitable sector and other vocations (e.g. open-source programming, academia, or the arts) is socially beneficial but not profitable, so people have to do it in their spare time, along with a traditional job. A basic income would allow these people to spend more time on work that is socially beneficial but unprofitable for the individual.

Increases number of people in jobs they enjoy. As people will not be forced to take on a job, they will be more able to find a job that they enjoy (or that pays well enough to offset their lack of enjoyment). Having people in jobs that suit them better will help to improve mental health, as well as leading to an improved quality of goods and services.

Gives financial independence to all adults. Every adult will be entitled to the basic income independently of any other people. This means they cannot be controlled or manipulated by someone through control of their finances, allowing people in abusive relationships to escape them more easily.[8]

Prevents generational theft. Most western countries already provide basic income to people of retired age. But, if a nation or its socialized retirement program goes bankrupt, or the socialized retirement program otherwise becomes unaffordable, in 20 or 30 years (due to fiscal mismanagement or simple birth rate demographics) then it is to the great advantage of current benefit recipients, and at the total cost to those who pay into the benefits today with the false promise of receiving them in the future. If entitlements are unaffordable/unsustainable, then the only fair solution is to provide the funds equally today.

Reduces the intensity of certain perverse economic incentives. When a person serves on jury duty, he or she faces a situation with perverse economic incentives: low-wage-earners are incentivized to drag out the case to continue receiving any jury-duty stipend, while high-wage-earners are incentivized to bring the case to a swift conclusion, so they can get back to work. Companies are incentivized to punish any salaried workers who sit on juries for a long time. All of these incentives lead to injustice within the judicial system and would be reduced if a person's income came less from their work and more from a basic income. More specifically, if a person currently makes a $20/hr. wage, sitting in a jury box is costing him $20/hr.; but after implementing a basic income, as funded by a 10% flat tax (for example), his after-tax wage is only $18/hr. (a loss which is offset by his basic income), so by sitting in a jury box he stands to lose less money than before. In general, any unpaid civic duty, such as jury duty, voting, democratic involvement, civil service, charity work, blood donation, etc., is supported by a basic income.

Leverages the multiplier effect.[9] "The mechanism that can give rise to a multiplier effect is that an initial incremental amount of spending can lead to increased consumption spending, increasing income further and hence further increasing consumption, etc., resulting in an overall increase in national income greater than the initial incremental amount of spending." It is this same effect that is seen in the differences to the economy the effects of $1 being spent by high income earners versus low income earners have. As published in a recent report, "All those dollars low-wage workers spend create an economic ripple effect. Every extra dollar going into the pockets of low-wage workers, standard economic multiplier models tell us, adds about $1.21 to the national economy. Every extra dollar going into the pockets of a high-income American, by contrast, only adds about 39 cents to the GDP."[10] This means a basic income could show this same multiplier effect on the entire economy by redistributing money from high earners to low and middle earners, where spending is amplified.

How much would the basic income be?

While many scholars argue that the basic income should be slightly below the minimum income needed to survive, many argue that a basic income must constitute a livable income in a viable post-automation society, on the grounds that a poverty level income is just that: still poverty. Such subjective guidelines have warranted a multitude of quantifications:

In 1969, the United States President's Commission on Income Maintenance Programs report, Poverty Amid Plenty: The American Paradox detailed a 1969 Basic Income Proposal[11] stated, "the Committee proposes providing a basic income of around $4,700 per adult and around $2,900 per child. So, for a family of four, it would be around $15,200 per year."[12] In 2014 US dollars, this equates to a basic income of $30,430[13] per adult U.S. citizen, $49,200[14] for a single parent, and $98,400[15] for a family of four.

The 2018 Alaska Permanent Fund amount is $1,600 per eligible citizen.[16] "To be eligible for a PFD, you must have been an Alaska resident for the entire calendar year preceding the date you apply for a dividend and intend to remain an Alaska resident indefinitely at the time you apply for a dividend."

Charles Murray in Guaranteed Income as a Replacement for the Welfare State introduced the figure of $10,000, "as a place to begin discussion,"[17] never really intending for it to be taken as a serious final number. "In the United States, a GI of $10,000 per year for all adults aged twenty-one years and older will cost no more than the projected cost of the current system as of 2011. By 2028, it will cost more than a trillion dollars less per year than the projected costs of the current system." Similarly, numbers just at or below the antiquated federal poverty level are generally considered illustrative rather than practical for legislative purposes.

Mark Walker in the February 2014 issue of the Journal of Evolution & Technology describes a plan for a $11,400 BIG paid to everyone ages 18 through 64 through the adoption of a 14% VAT (Value Added Tax).[18] According to Walker, "The vast majority would do better under this proposal even though it includes a large new tax: anyone making between $0 and $80,000 a year would be monetarily better off. About 90% of the population has a net personal income that falls below the crossover point (U.S. Department of Commerce, 2014). So, the vast majority of the population would be better off financially under the 14% VAT and BIG proposal.

Ed Dolan has calculated that the US could afford a basic income of $5,850[19] (paid to everyone, including children) if it got rid of most means tested benefits and tax exemptions for the middle classes. If children were excluded, this figure would rise to $7647.

In 2005, the BIG Pilot Project in Namibia began as the result of the proposal that, "A monthly cash grant of not less than N$100 (~13 US$) should be paid to every Namibian."[20] Here we begin to see the concept of local context emerge. Indexing basic income to the real economy is vital to its credibility and viability.

The 2013 Swiss basic income guarantee referendum, the first of its scale and kind in the twenty-first century, was for CHF ₣2,500 francs (approximately USD $2,800/mo.)[21] equivalent to $33,600 USD per year.[22] Albert Jorimann (president of BIEN Switzerland) says about that: "We refer in the collection of signatures to effectively 2500 CHF per adult, which could actually be something like a little over 2000 euros. However, one must consider the cost of living, which are significantly higher in Switzerland than in the EU. Here (in Switzerland) a 4-room apartment quickly ends up costing 2500 francs, and not only in the big cities. So, I would equate the amount in euros rather with about 1000 euros" Dutch Basic Income Website.[23]

reddit.com/r/BasicIncome/wiki/

In the United States, using the 2014 Federal Poverty Guidelines as a guide,[24] to universally prevent poverty would require a basic income level of $12,000 (also considered an appropriate amount using a ground up analysis)[25] for everyone over the age of 18, along with a partial basic income of $4,000 for everyone under the age of 18. According to /u/2noame,[26] this particular plan would require $2.98 trillion in total revenue ($2.7 trillion for 18+ and $276 billion for 18-) to cover all U.S. citizens, or after the elimination of current government pensions and welfare programs, $1.28 trillion USD.

As of August 2014, Cato Institute's Michael Tanner (PDF),[27] calculates that adding "another $284 of welfare spending [to existing federal welfare alone] at the state and local level, and you've got almost $1 trillion dollars of government spending on welfare - over $20,000 for every poor person in the United States (Zwolinski, Matt. The Pragmatic Libertarian Case for a Basic Income Guarantee).[28]

The Socialist Alternative 2014 party platform includes, "A minimum guaranteed weekly income of $600/week (~$28,800/yr.) for the unemployed, disabled, stay-at-home parents, the elderly, and others unable to work."[29]

Any meaningful basic income figure must respond to changes in livable incomes for the locale in which it is instituted. It should not be an arbitrarily-decided static number which fails to be revisited and updated over time. One alternative is to set the basic income level as a fixed percentage of median income (for the five years 2009-2013, 50% of US median income average is $26,523)[30] or of per capita GDP (in 2014, 50% of US GDP/capita is $27,650)[31]. Another idea is to have congress periodically vote on the basic income: each congressman proposes a desired value, and the median proposal is used for the next year. If implemented by the states, state congresses would vote.

Higher levels of basic income than discussed above are possible; for a discussion of how additional revenue could be raised, see the "How Would You Pay For It" section.

If you want to play with the numbers yourself, /u/JayDurst made a calculator,[32] that would allow you to look at different tax rates and the basic income rate that you could afford with it (discussion here).[33]

The "law of rent" says that more money in the hands of the people causes inflation in natural resource leasing costs (rent, resource extraction (mining), wireless communication frequencies, geosynchronous orbits, etc.), which could entirely eliminate the original benefit of a basic income for non-land-owners. But if basic income is partially funded with a Georgist land value tax (LVT), those rent increases get returned right back to the basic-income recipients who boosted the value of the land in the first place. A socialist system like this, or a capitalist system in which citizens typically hold diversified land portfolios, can mitigate the harmful effects of rent inflation.

Is this similar to a negative income tax?

A negative income tax is a proposal to include negative rates of income tax for people earning below a certain level.[34] A level of income would be set at which you pay zero tax; if you earn more than this you pay tax, but if you earn less you would receive payments. Like basic income, this would not have any conditions (e.g. having to work to get the payment) but unlike basic income, the payments are dependent on income. However, a negative income tax can be set up so that it provides the same amount of money as a basic income. This is because a basic income scheme would require higher tax rates than a negative income tax, as it involves paying every citizen. A NIT would have lower tax rates but provide less money, so these two could balance out in such a way that every citizen has the same amount of money that they would with a basic income. There are pros and cons to both approaches:[35] a basic income would involve giving money to people who don't need it, which people might consider unfair even though they are repaying the money through their tax, while a negative income tax could lead to stigmatization of people who receive payments, as the payments would not be universal. A negative income tax also appeals to those who care more about negative liberty (freedom from others),[36] while unconditional basic income appeals to those care more about positive liberty (freedom to do what you want).[37]

That's all very well, but where's the evidence?

Experiments with unconditional cash benefits around the world have often proven to be one of the most successful ways of reducing poverty, and in the vast majority of cases, the fear that people would waste their money on drugs or alcohol, become lazy, or have more kids were not realized,[38] and were even reduced.[39] Experimental studies and wider programs and pilots have taken place in:

- Manitoba, Canada (The "Mincome" Experiment)[40]
- Seattle and Denver (SIME & DIME)[41]
- North Carolina and rural Iowa (RIME)[42]
- Gary, Indiana (GIME)[43]
- New Jersey (NJIME)[44]
- Alaska (Alaskan PFD)[45] with (2018 study showing 17% increase in PT employment)[46]

reddit.com/r/BasicIncome/wiki/

- Namibia (BIG Pilot Project)[47] (link to full report)[48]
- Namibia (Emergency Cash Grant)[49]
- India (Madhya Pradesh Pilots)[50] (link to full report)[51]
- Win for Life lottery winners (€1,000/month)[52]
- Bomi County, Liberia (SCT Programme)[53]
- Lebanon (WCAP)[54]
- Brazil (Bolsa Familia)[55]
- Brazil (Quatinga Velho)[56]
- Kenya (GiveDirectly)[57]
- Kenya (Hunger Safety Net Program)[58]
- Uganda (WINGS)[59]
- Uganda (NUSAF's Youth Opportunities Program (YOP))[60]
- Eastern Band of Cherokee Indians in North Carolina (Casino revenue)[61]
- London,[62] *Hough, Juliette, and Becky Rice. "Providing personalized support to rough sleepers."[63] York, JRF (2010).
- New York City[64]
- Iran,[65] (link to 2017 study on labor supply effects)[66] (link to 2018 study on labor supply effects)[67] (note: increased employment for women and self-employment for men)

- Berkshire, UK (in 1795)[68]
- Liberia slums (drug users and criminals)[69]
- Mexico's Programa de Apoyo Alimentario (note: no observed inflation)[70] (link to paper)[71]
- Canada's Healthy Baby Prenatal Benefit (note: no strings cash resulted in babies born healthier)[72]
- Democratic Republic of Congo.[73]
- Malawi (note: decreased pregnancy rates)[74]
- Kuwait in 2011 (note: increased non-oil GDP through higher consumer spending)[75]
- Zambia (note: after 3 yrs. households had 59% more to spend than amount received)[76]
- US Social Security natural experiment (note: more money caused increased cognitive function)[77] (link to paper)[78]
- Longitudinal study of 1,000 people for 35 years (note: childhood impoverishment leads to greater addictions, worse health, and more crimes as adults)[79]
- Mothers' Pension program (US 1911-1935) (note: longer life, more education, healthier weights, earned more income)[80]
- Pakistan's Citizens Damage Compensation Program ("Watan Card") (note: lower declines in aspirations for the future)[81]

reddit.com/r/BasicIncome/wiki/

- Dolly Parton's My People Fund (note: $1,000 per month considered more helpful than any other form of support by those displaced by Gatlinburg fires)[82]
- An easy to read summary of these studies is included,[83] in addition to more Experimental Summary Papers:
- Basic Income Programs and Pilots.[84]
- Universal Basic Income: A New Tool for Development Policy.[85]

Who supports the basic income guarantee?

Basic income, and the similar proposal of a negative income tax, have a range of supporters from across the political spectrum.[86] Some of these supporters and links to their arguments in favor of basic income are given below. A growing number of today's best thinkers are rapidly joining the long history of leading thinkers in advocating this policy.

Nobel prize winning economists:

- Paul Krugman,[87] @NYTimeskrugman.[88]
- Milton Friedman.[89]
- F. A. Hayek.[90]
- Herbert A. Simon.[91]
- James Meade.[92]
- Robert Solow.[93]

- James Mirrlees.[94]
- Christopher Pissarides.[95]

Other economists:

- Yanis Varoufakis (Former Greek Minister of Finance)[96]
- Umair Haque,[97] @umairh,[98] (Harvard Business School Economist)
- Recent Mentions: "it's a no-brainer"[99] | "the next big social issue"[100] | "but it'll never happen"[101] | if WE don't make it happen.
- Erik Brynjolfsson, @erikbryn,[102] (MIT Economist, Author, "Race Against the Machine")
- J. K. Galbraith (American economist)[103]
- Robert Skidelsky (Skip to the section "Working Less") (Economic historian and professor emeritus of political economy)[104]
- Guy Standing,[105] (video: Why the Precariat Requires a Basic Income)[106] (British economist)
- Daniel Raventos (Spanish economist)[107]
- Ed Dolan.[108]

Philosophers:

- Bertrand Russell (see the last paragraph of chapter IV for a summary)[109]

reddit.com/r/BasicIncome/wiki/

- John Stuart Mill (Chapter I: Of Property § 4) (British philosopher)[110]
- Thomas Paine.[111]
- Philippe Van Parijs (Philosopher and left-libertarian economist)[112]
- Alan Watts.[113]

Politicians and Activists:

- Martin Luther King Jr. (American pastor, activist, and leader in the African-American Civil Rights Movement)[114] (also video)[115]
- Desmond Tutu (former Archbishop of Cape Town, South Africa, and anti-apartheid activist; winner of the Nobel Peace Prize in 1984)[116]
- Robert Reich (former United States Secretary of Labor)[117]
- Charles Murray [PDF] (American libertarian political scientist)[118]
- Hugh Segal (Canadian political commentator and former senator)[119]
- Charles Eisenstein,[120] (video: "A BI gives us the freedom to act on our desire to give")[121]
- Edward Snowden (former NSA contractor who leaked information about their overbearing surveillance practices)[122]
- Peter Joseph, founder of the Zeitgeist Movement,[123] (video interview about UBI)[124]

- Ralph Nader (Green Party and Independent presidential candidate)[125]
- Federico Pistono (author of Robots Will Steal Your Job, But That's OK)[126]
- Bernie Sanders (Junior US Senator D-VT)[127]

Health professionals:

- The Canadian Medical Association (Delegates' Motion 5-16, page 11, or pdf page 18)[128]
- 194 Ontario physicians.[129]

You can read more about basic income supporters from the past 240 years, on the European Unconditional Basic Income website, UBIE.ORG.[130]

I believe in [insert ideology]. Why should I support a basic income guarantee?

The following brief arguments are taken verbatim from this article,[131] which provides various arguments from different political perspectives.

Fairness

Property is a social construct legally enforced by the government. If all people are considered equal, then absent any other considerations, each person should have an equal amount of property. So material equality should be the default. In a free market economy with a basic income at or below the highest sustainable rate, those who choose to live off of the basic income are not living off of the work of others. Rather, they are living off of less than their "fair share" of property and allowing the extra to be used by those who choose to work.

Utilitarianism

The free market is the greatest generator of wealth ever devised. Money is the most effective means of socially producing utility, as it allows each individual to obtain whatever needs and wants they subjectively require. However, one dollar in the hands of a poorer person produces greater utility than a dollar in the hands of a richer person, because the richer person can fulfill more of their more important needs and wants with the rest of their money than the poorer person can. So, the transfer of money from a richer person to a poorer person increases overall utility. The government is incompetent at running people's lives or regulating the economy, but the one thing it can do effectively is mail out checks. A basic income is most effective means of transferring money from the richer to the poorer with the least government interference and the least work disincentive. The natural limit on the amount of the basic income is the point where the work disincentive from the required taxes reduces wealth the point where the basic income would have to be reduced.

Keynesianism

Keynesian economics works when implemented correctly. But properly implementing Keynesian economics is politically very difficult. It requires politicians who are willing to spend a lot of money on stimulus when the government appears broke, and then turn around and become deficit hawks when the government is rolling in cash and everyone wants a piece of the pie. A basic income funded primarily from an income tax would become a massive institutionalized entitlement expected by the population whose cost would automatically increase and decrease in direct opposition to the economy. As unemployment rises, the number of net receivers goes up, and as unemployment falls, so will the number of net receivers. Keynes once famously said that the government should pay people to dig holes and fill them back up again. But why waste people's time? Anyone who sits on the couch and watches TV while living off of a basic income will contribute as much to society as the hole diggers. And anyone who does anything more productive will create a net good for society.

Human Rights

Poverty is not a natural tragedy like cancer or earthquakes. Poverty is a human caused tragedy like slavery or government oppression. Slavery is caused by societal recognition of humans as property. Government oppression is caused by governments punishing people for their beliefs or characteristics, and without due process of law. Poverty is caused by property laws that deny some people access to necessities. These types of tragedies can be ended by recognizing that humans have the right not to be subjected to tortuous conditions imposed by other humans. Humans have a right not to live in slavery. Humans have a right to be free of government oppression. And humans have a right not to live in poverty. A basic income is not a strategy for dealing with poverty; it is the elimination of poverty. The campaign for a basic income is a campaign for the abolition of poverty. It is the abolitionist movement of the 21st century.

Georgism/Geolibertarianism

Property is a product of creation, not of mere use. "I made this." confers property rights, "Tag! It's mine!" does not. Things that exist as a product of your labor must be yours, and for anyone else to appropriate them is to make you their slave. Land and natural resources, however, are not the products of people, but of nature or God. They are gifts to all of humanity. Individual property in land and natural resources may be practical or useful, but it is still theft. Utility might justify this theft, but compensation is still required. As the appropriation was done without consent, the compensation must be in the form that offers the greatest choice of use to the victims. That form is cash. The most efficient arrangement for payment is for the takers to pay the full rental or use value to a single entity which can then divide the proceeds equally among the population. Taxes are the tribute I pay to you for displacing you from land, the basic income is your dividend.

Transhumanism/Futurology

Two hundred thousand years ago humans lived in hunter-gatherer societies. About 10 thousand years ago, humans began to live in agricultural societies, and then about 300 years ago, humans began to live in industrial societies. Since 30 to 50 years ago, we have lived in a service society. Theoretically, the last economic stage of society is a leisure society, where most people either work in the artistic or scientific fields, or do not work at all. So far, each phase has lasted only a small fraction of the time of the previous phase. If that pattern holds, service societies should last less than two generations, a time period nearing its end. Right now, worker productivity is advancing faster than the need for workers, and robots are inhabiting labs in research hospitals and at DARPA. It is time to prepare for a society in which we simply do not need everyone to work. A basic income will be needed to provide a living for people, and to provide customers for business.

Conservatism

The welfare state may not be the society we would have created, but it has been here for 4 generations, people have come to expect and rely on it, and it would be extremely disruptive to society to get rid of it. But while we may not be able to get rid of the welfare state, we can reform it. The current welfare state necessitates an immense and expensive bureaucracy, it is prohibitively complicated for some of its intended beneficiaries to navigate, it puts bureaucrats in charge of the lives of the poor, it creates perverse incentives for people to avoid work and to remain poor, and it arbitrarily allows some people to fall through the cracks. A basic income would correct all of these problems. A basic income is simple to administer, treats all people equally, retains all rewards for hard work, savings, and entrepreneurship, and trusts the poor to make their own decisions about what to do with their money, taking these decisions out of the hands of paternalistic elitist politicians.

Socialism

While a UBI won't lead us straight into a worker-owned, democratic economy like what a socialist would advocate for, you would find that many socialists advocate for a UBI because it satisfies one of the biggest tenets of socialism; collective efforts from society that would benefit all of society, which by any means could mean heavier taxation that goes right back to the community equally. This is why Marx was such a heavy advocate for the public-school system, and prominent socialists like MLK supported a movement that would limit the socio-economic disparity between Whites and Blacks. While Public Schools and Equality aren't socialism (since they don't lead us to worker-owned cooperatives), they are definitely socialist, and intrinsically socialist, because they are all necessary to socialism. It also becomes evident that a UBI would guarantee that people wouldn't be tied down to profit for their entire lives. In his "Base and Superstructure" Theory, Marx mentioned how it was the "Base" (the economic means and distribution of production) that affected the "Superstructure" (the relationship between people and the economy and general mindset of it, etc.). With a UBI, an artist or a scientist wouldn't have to be tied down by profit in order to innovate or express themselves, individuals would be given the time and opportunity to do as they please, and in turn give back to the community not for the purpose of profit, but for the purpose of contribution in the field they feel they have an interest in be it sports, physical work, art, etc.

Feminism

Patriarchy has put the world's wealth in the hands of men, prevented women from being professionals and entrepreneurs, forced poor women into dead-end second-class labor jobs, and forced all women to become unpaid domestic servants and caretakers of the young, elderly, and disabled of their families. Women have been forced to be financially dependent on fathers or husbands who are often abusive. A basic income would change all of this. A basic income would be a massive transfer of wealth from men to women. Women would be free of financial dependence on any man, and the young, elderly, and disabled would all be fully supported. Women could afford to leave abusive husbands, those who chose to be caretakers would be fully compensated, and no woman would be forced into a dead-end job, and would instead be able to pursue her own financial goals as she saw fit.

Libertarianism

The most common form of government oppression in practice today is obfuscation of the law through complexity. The tax code is needlessly complex. Social

Security, Medicaid, Welfare and Medicare are massive bureaucracies that not only coerce citizens out of their money, but can make it difficult for anyone but bureaucrats to retrieve the proper benefits guaranteed them. In most cases, citizens simply have to live with whatever payments the government decides is proper, whether it be from entitlement programs or via tax refunds.

A Basic Income program would eliminate massive bureaucracies. Most Basic Income proposals come coupled with a restructuring of the tax code to simplify it - most often in the form of a flat tax. Basic Income proposals also usually call for the replacement of existing entitlement programs. Government entities running means-tested programs will vanish. The government will no longer have a need to look into the bank accounts of private citizens or check their medical records before making payments. Every citizen simply gets a check in the mail once a month.

While a Basic Income calls for an increase in taxes and spending, it also comes with a massive reduction in the size of government, which means more liberty for everyone. Basic Income is one of the rare government social programs that actually decreases the influence of government and furthers the cause of liberty.

reddit.com/r/BasicIncome/wiki/

Liberalism/Social Democracy

A basic income would correct or ameliorate many inequities and inefficiencies inherent in market capitalism. The wages of unskilled and semi-skilled workers would rise as those who enjoy and are good at such work will no longer have to compete against those who are forced to seek such work out of financial necessity. The wages of highly skilled workers will fall as more people are able to take the time necessary to gain the skills to compete for those jobs, lowering the cost of legal, financial, and health care services. A guaranteed income will soften the blow to workers displaced by advancing technology and the creative destruction of the market. Job seekers will be able to take the time necessary to find work that is the best fit for them, increasing efficiency in the distribution of labor. And entrepreneurship will flourish as those wanting to start their own businesses will have an income to survive on during the long lean times that typically come when building a new enterprise.

Environmentalism

Technological unemployment is often described as the result of an inexorable march toward further sophistication, but perhaps it can be better understood as being the result of high labor costs combined with minimal penalties for damaging the environment.

Economists have long advocated reducing carbon emissions and other environmental damage by simply levying taxes (or penalties) upon such activities. As of now, this approach has largely been rejected by the political establishment due to the regressive economic effects of increased living costs. However, these effects could be eliminated if the proceeds from taxation of environmental damage were used to increase the UBI.

Workers may be willing to work for lower wages if the UBI already provides them enough to live on. This effect will be particularly amplified for rewarding, self-actualizing professions. Conversely, high labor costs encourage more automation and electricity consumption, as well as favoring further resource extraction over recycling, reuse and repair. This results in significant environmental externalities. Cheap labor, especially when combined with consumption taxes, will reduce our economic dependency upon continued environmental exploitation.

What are the arguments against basic income?

There is an ongoing collection of articles and blogs against the idea available in this subreddit for study, which can be accessed by using the "Anti-UBI"[132] search filter in the sidebar. Most arguments tend to come down to: "Taxation is theft" (even though taxation isn't required), "Everyone will stop working" (even though all data points to the contrary), and "By replacing all government services, basic income will leave people worse off" (even though basic income is only intended to replace many -- not all -- government programs and services).

How would you pay for it?

First and foremost, the basic income is paid for by direct savings of eliminating the waste, fraud, and abuse of the Welfare State. Charles Murray writes, "After a process that has taken decades, the welfare state has severely degraded the traditions of work, thrift, and neighborliness which enabled the system to work at the outset. It is now spawning social and economic problems that it is powerless to solve."[133]

By completely ending welfare as we know it, "In the United States, a GI (guaranteed income) for all adults aged twenty-one years and older will cost no more than the projected cost of the current system as of 2011. By 2028, [the guaranteed income] will cost a trillion dollars less per year than the projected costs of the current system." Not all would like to go so far as Charles Murray however, and instead believe it would make more sense to keep certain universal government services, like healthcare and education for example.

Secondly, the complete elimination of the Minimum Wage and all associated payroll overheard for businesses. The reason for a basic income that is a fully guaranteed, realistic, living income (see 'How much would the basic income be?') indexed to the real economy is so that these cost savings can all be fully realized and redeployed toward empowering innovation (Christensen).

Of course, taxes on high-end consumption and financial transactions are currently two of the leading methods proposed to make up any gap between the savings gained in completely dismantling the current means-tested welfare state, and a sustainable basic income. Means-testing is a breeding ground for fraud and abuse in any program, and welfare is not immune.[134] Some argue that waste, fraud, and abuse is so understated and invisible, that the gap between savings in total welfare elimination and basic income could be much smaller than presently calculated.

The general idea of fundraising is via taxation. Just as current welfare systems use tax revenue to fund subsidies, the basic income would as well. A simple setup is just a flat tax on income,[135] and/or a flat sales tax. There are a variety of other taxes that could help to fund basic income, depending on the desired secondary effects of the tax. Many European countries use a value added tax (VAT)[136] to positive effect without materially harming consumption. A carbon tax would help to combat global warming as well as providing a new revenue source for basic income. A tax on High Frequency Traders ("Robin Hood tax")[137] would reduce market "flash crashes" without materially harming market efficiency, and a transaction tax on all electronic transactions (APT tax)[138] would tiny per transaction but massive in aggregate. A wealth tax could be more effective in reducing inequality than a traditional income tax. A land value tax (LVT)[139] - taxing the owners of land for its value, excluding any man-made developments on it - would cause very little economic distortion while raising revenue. Many wealthy people earn more from capital gains than income, so raising the level of capital gains tax is likely to produce a lot of revenue. Inheritance tax helps to fight the unfairness of people born to rich parents having a head start in life. And of course, simply raising income tax is always an option.

Recognizing the existence of our common wealth - the property that no one ever made, or we all make together - and charging for its use is another method. This is what's known as the "Alaska Model,"[140] because it would be similar to how Alaska funds its dividends for all residents, but it would be extended to all the many other common resources like water, air, the electromagnetic spectrum, Big Data, etc. It has been estimated by Peter Barnes that this method can alone provide everyone in the US $5,000 per year.[141]

One other possibility is to include the funding of basic income with citizen centered monetary policy.[142]

In a recession, if interest rates are very low and inflation is not too high, but the economy is not growing, the central bank will essentially print money to help increase demand. This has happened in the current crisis; the US Federal Reserve between 2009 and 2014 added $5 trillion to the money supply in quantitative easing (QE)[143]. So, in certain circumstances, the central bank could print money and cover some of the cost of the basic income for the government, meaning that the government will be free to either cut taxes or increase spending to stimulate the economy without adding to its deficit.

Basically, there are all sorts of underused ways to raise revenue for basic income. No one tax would be able to completely pay for it, but a combination of the different taxes discussed above, as well as the savings from dismantling the current welfare bureaucracy, make it more affordable than it appears. There are a number of studies which have proposed more detailed costed proposals for basic income in the United States,[144] UK,[145] Ireland,[146] among others.

No matter how the revenue is raised however, the origins of its surplus ultimately comes from one place, and that place is the same reason the majority of our efforts no longer goes into food production, but into the 98% of our economic activity that now involves everything else. And that is the machine. The machine pays for it.[147]

Exactly which government programs could be cut with basic income in place?

Some examples of programs that become obsolete/optional depending on the amount of UBI, once implemented:

- welfare/workfare
- tax deductions/credits/subsidies
- unemployment insurance
- government pensions
- disability benefits
- national minimum wage laws

The beneficiaries of these programs would receive their UBI cash in place of the above benefits. This has the advantage of increasing beneficiaries' liberty and eliminating most bureaucratic overhead.

Note: The above programs need not be all or nothing. For example, disability and pensions can exist in smaller forms on top of UBI and still reduce overhead costs.

Allan Sheahen's proposal for a basic income in the United States includes in its appendix a list of 138 tax loopholes that could be closed to help pay for the UBI,[148] as well as over 100 federal programs that could be eliminated as being unnecessary with basic income. For a list of all federal government funded programs in the United States, see this collection of 1,607 programs dated 2005,[149] many of which could be seen as redundant or unnecessary after introduction of basic income.

Wouldn't basic income just cause inflation?

This question arises so much, this article,[150] by Scott Santens has been written to answer it from a variety of perspectives. If you want a much greater understanding of basic income and inflation, please read it in its entirety.

There is no current consensus on just to what degree a basic income would impact prices. The ongoing concern from detractors that inflation would reduce the effectiveness of any BI payment, delivering less net benefit than intended, exists despite the lack of evidence to support this concern. Assuming the BI is funded by taxes, and not monetary policy (printing money), the inflationary impact should be short-term and limited to where supply is sticky.

Monetary Economics

The quantity theory of money links long-term inflation tightly with the money supply,[151] of which the basic income has no direct impact (assuming the BI is not funded via monetary means). This could suggest that, in the long-term, the BI would have no real impact on inflation.

Alaska Permanent Fund

Alaska has operated what is essentially a miniature Basic Income program that has paid out annually since 1982,[152] where the only restrictions on receivers are residency requirements and various ineligibility rules for criminal actions. Alaska has experienced lower levels of inflation compared to the U.S. average since the inception of the program.[153]

Other Thoughts

Basic income may impact inflation via a rise in compensation costs for businesses. If the labor force shrinks after the introduction of a basic income businesses may have to bid up compensation in order to attract and retain workers, or make capital investments in order to automate work previously done by people.

An increase in aggregate demand as a result of the basic income could impact short-term prices of goods and services when productive capacity is at 100% and where the supply is sticky as a result of spending patterns (XLS spreadsheet)[154] of lower income households. Since lower income households tend to spend the majority of their income a large portion of the Basic Income going to low income households would be spent. However, since the Basic Income is designed to replace most current government transfers, the increase in demand may be muted.

For more discussion, here are some threads from this subreddit talking about basic income's effect on prices:

- www.reddit.com/r/BasicIncome/comments/1r8nbz/question_from_an_outside_who_just_stumbled_upon/
- www.reddit.com/r/BasicIncome/comments/1sicrc/how_could_inflation_caused_by_implementation_of/
- www.reddit.com/r/BasicIncome/comments/1qlo3e/how_will_basic_income_affect_inflation_any/
- www.reddit.com/r/BasicIncome/comments/1petz4/wouldnt_basic_income_crash_a_countries_economy/
- www.reddit.com/r/BasicIncome/comments/1t4fol/ubis_effect_on_housing_market/
- www.reddit.com/r/BasicIncome/comments/1mvqfl/econ_101_and_basic_income/

reddit.com/r/BasicIncome/wiki/

What's the point of giving money to the high-earners? Why not target it only at the poor?

Giving money to all people equally completely removes the problematic unemployment/poverty trap (see list of benefits above). Another benefit of this is that if everyone receives the payment, cutting the basic income will reduce everyone's income; thus, changes to the UBI amount would be far less politicized. Giving money to everyone also greatly reduces administration costs and simplifies the scheme, as you don't have to check someone's income to determine their UBI allowance. Finally, high-earners would be paying more in taxes than they were getting from their basic income, so in net terms the rich are still paying while the poor benefit.

What about variations in the cost of living? Wouldn't major cities need much more money than rural areas?

Most discussions about basic income and the cost of living (for example this one)[155] favor making no adjustments. With a basic income people will be more able to move to cheaper areas, as they don't have to worry about having a job immediately when they get there. Adjusting for the cost of living would greatly increase the administration required for basic income (how do you determine where people are living, or the exact amount that you should adjust the basic income by?), which negates one of the main benefits of it. Of course, local governments would be free to introduce additional welfare that would lower the cost of living for the poor, but this would be separate from any national basic income scheme.

Isn't this communism?

No. Have a look at the list of supporters, for one thing – Milton Friedman and F. A. Hayek would not support communism! Communism, by definition, is a revolutionary socialist movement to create a classless, moneyless and stateless social order structured upon common ownership of the means of production. Basic income is not revolutionary (in that it doesn't need a revolution to happen), does not require the eradication of classes, does not require the eradication of the state, and doesn't require common ownership of the means of production. So it is not communism; it is merely a socialist correction to capitalism, thus allowing capitalism to continue to prevail over the domains in which it excels (finding appropriate prices and quantities of tangible and some intangible goods/services).

reddit.com/r/BasicIncome/wiki/

This sounds interesting. Where can I find out more?

Reddit-style FAQ

- Comprehensive list of Basic Income questions, and discussion.[156]

Mainstream media coverage

- The Economist.[157]
- BBC.[158]
- New York Times.[159]
- Financial Times (mirror of paywalled article).[160]
- USA Today.[161]
- Fox News.[162]
- Washington Post,[163] (an abridged reprint of this excellent article from De Correspondent).[164]
- CNN.[165]
- PBS.[166]
- Huffington Post.[167]
- Newsweek.[168]
- Scientific American.[169]

Extended audio/video discussions

- Milton Friedman talking about negative income tax.[170]

- Guy Standing giving a lecture about basic income.[171]
- Philippe van Parijs giving a lecture about basic income.[172]
- David Graeber and Barbara Jacobson discussing basic income.[173]
- A documentary created for the Swiss basic income initiative, in German with English subtitles.[174]

Blog posts

- FiveThirtyEight (article).[175]
- A series of posts from Economonitor: What are the economic arguments for basic income,[176] could we afford it,[177] different political perspectives on it.[178]
- Various posts from Pieria: Creative destruction, basic income and the jobs of the future.[179]

Books

- Amazon Listmania list by /u/2noame,180 of 40 books to read about or involving a basic income guarantee.[181]

Academic Papers

- Basic Income Earth Network's list of Papers and Resources.[182]

reddit.com/r/BasicIncome/wiki/

This sounds great! What can I do to make it happen?

- See the What can I do to support basic income?[183]
- Another good place to start would be to join one of the many advocacy groups around the world,[184] or join a city-level meetup group.[185]
- It's also very simple to contact your local politician or local newspaper, to press the case for Basic Income or an article on the subject.[186]
- You can also advocate for Basic Income online by using the #BasicIncome hashtag and sharing updates from these social media accounts.[187]
- It's been shown that ideas spread most effectively from family members and friends, so start talking about Basic Income to everyone you know!

FAQ References

1.
www.basicincome.org/bien/aboutbasicincome.html

2. www.un.org/en/universal-declaration-human-rights/index.html

3.
www.sciencemag.org/content/341/6149/976.abstract

4. basicincome.org.uk/interview/2013/08/health-forget-mincome-poverty/

5. [1.]
www.nytimes.com/2013/06/14/opinion/krugman-sympathy-for-the-luddites.html?hpw&_r=1& [2.]
www.technologyreview.com/featuredstory/515926/how-technology-is-destroying-jobs/

6.
thecurrentmoment.files.wordpress.com/2011/08/productivity-and-real-wages.jpg

7.
www.policyinnovations.org/ideas/briefings/data/000163

8.
www.jstor.org/discover/10.2307/2778257?uid=3739736&uid=2&uid=4&
uid=3739256&sid= 21104536671703

9. en.wikipedia.org/wiki/Fiscal_multiplier

reddit.com/r/BasicIncome/wiki/

10. www.ips-dc.org/reports/wall_street_bonuses_and_the_minimum_wage

11. www.demos.org/blog/2/3/14/poverty-amid-plenty-1969-basic-income-proposal

12. books.google.com/books/about/Poverty_amid_plenty_the_American_paradox.html?id= T9AtAAAAMAAJ&redir_esc=y

13. wolfr.am/1alx3qz

14. wolfr.am/1fI4pzc

15. wolfr.am/1inEqhq

16. pfd.alaska.gov/

17. www.fljs.org/sites/www.fljs.org/files/publications/Murray.pdf

18. jetpress.org/v24/walker.htm

19. www.economonitor.com/dolanecon/2014/01/13/could-we-afford-a-universal-basic-income/

20. bignam.org/BIG_pilot.html

21. wolfr.am/1e3k7TV

22. www.bbc.co.uk/news/business-25415501

23. basisinkomen.nl/wp/2500-zwitserse-frank-is-hier-maar-1000-euro-waard-en-geen-2080/

24. familiesusa.org/product/federal-poverty-guidelines

25. hawkins.ventures/post/85265679392/what-is-an-appropriate-level-of-basic-income

26. www.reddit.com/r/BasicIncome/comments/25g34u/cmv_we_cannot_
afford_ubi/ chh3s5n

27. www.cato.org/sites/cato.org/files/pubs/pdf/PA694.pdf

28. www.cato-unbound.org/2014/08/04/matt-zwolinski/pragmatic-libertarian-case-basic-income-guarantee

29. www.socialistalternative.org/about/

30. www.wolframalpha.com/input/?i=50%25+of+US+median+income

31. As of 2018, this figure has risen to $31,129, further proving efficacy of this indexing principle. www.wolframalpha.com/input/?i=united+states+gdp+per+capita+*+.5

32. [1.]www.reddit.com/u/JayDurst [2.] jsfiddle.net/9nRZK/153/

33. www.reddit.com/r/BasicIncome/comments/1nzi9x/u

pdated_basic_income_
calculator _jsfiddle/

34. en.wikipedia.org/wiki/Negative_income_tax

35. mpra.ub.uni-
muenchen.de/7016/1/MPRA_paper_7016.pdf

36. en.wikipedia.org/wiki/Negative_liberty

37. en.wikipedia.org/wiki/Positive_liberty

38. blogs.worldbank.org/impactevaluations/do-
poor-waste-transfers-booze-and-cigarettes-no

39.
www.journals.uchicago.edu/doi/abs/10.1086/689575

40. basicincome.org.uk/interview/2013/08/health-
forget-mincome-poverty/

41.
www.bostonfed.org/economic/conf/conf30/conf30a.
pdf

42. irp.wisc.edu/publications/sr/pdfs/sr10.pdf

43. www.chicagomag.com/city-life/October-
2014/Want-to-Help-Gary-Indiana-Why-Not-Just-
Give-Them-Money/

44.
irp.wisc.edu/research/nit/NIT_index.htm#New%20J
ersey

45.
www.iser.uaa.alaska.edu/Publications/bien_xiii_ak
_pfd_lessons.pdf

46.
papers.ssrn.com/sol3/papers.cfm?abstract_id=31183
43

47.
www.policyinnovations.org/ideas/briefings/data/00
0163

48.
www.bignam.org/Publications/BIG_Assessment_re
port_08b.pdf

49.
www.bignam.org/Publications/Relief_through_cash
_Impact_assessment_
of_the_emergency _cash_grant_in_Namibia.pdf

50.
www.developmentpathways.co.uk/resources/wp-
content/uploads/2016/04/Indias-Basic-Income-
Experiment-PP21.pdf

51. sewabharat.org/wp-
content/uploads/2015/07/Report-on-Unconditional-
Cash-Transfer-Pilot-Project-in-Madhya-
Pradesh.pdf

52.
www.basicincome.org/bien/pdf/2004MarxPeeters.pd
f

53.
www.unicef.org/evaldatabase/files/Final_Evaluation

reddit.com/r/BasicIncome/wiki/

_of_SCT_Pilot_
Program _Liberia.pdf

54. www.rescue.org/sites/default/files/resource-file/Emergency%20Economies%20Evaluation%20Report%20FINAL%2009.09.14%20%282%29.pdf

55. motherboard.vice.com/blog/how-giving-cash-directly-to-the-poor-paid-off-in-brazil

56. binews.org/2012/06/brazil-basic-income-in-quatinga-velho-celebrates-3-years-of-operation/

57. www.givedirectly.org/blog_post.php?id=7156273363730338864

58. www.reuters.com/article/us-kenya-aid-idUSKBN0NW0C120150511

59. www.logica-wb.org/PDFs/LOGICA_StudySeriesNo1_Uganda_hr.pdf

60. cega.berkeley.edu/assets/cega_events/53/WGAPE_Sp2013_Blattman.pdf

61. opinionator.blogs.nytimes.com/2014/01/18/what-happens-when-the-poor-receive-a-stipend/?_r=0

62. www.economist.com/node/17420321

63. www.housingeurope.eu/file/261/download

64. www.mdrc.org/news/press-release/new-findings-show-new-york-city's-conditional-cash-transfer-initiative-reduced

65. www.bien2012.org/sites/default/files/paper_156_en.pdf

66. erf.org.eg/wp-content/uploads/2017/05/1090.pdf

67. www.sciencedirect.com/science/article/pii/S0304387818306084

68. www.pieria.co.uk/articles/an_experiment_with_basic_income

69. zunia.org/post/show-them-the-money-why-giving-cash-helps-alleviate-poverty

70. www.vox.com/policy-and-politics/2017/9/20/16256240/mexico-cash-transfer-inflation-basic-income

71. www.povertyactionlab.org/sites/default/files/publications/467_The-Price-Effect-of-Cash-versus-In-kind-Transfers_July%202017.pdf

72. www.cbc.ca/beta/news/health/healthy-baby-prenatal-income-benefit-1.3578029

reddit.com/r/BasicIncome/wiki/

73. www.cgdev.org/publication/cash-or-coupons-testing-impacts-cash-versus-vouchers-democratic-republic-congo-working

74. web.archive.org/web/20100612133719/irps.ucsd.edu/assets/037/11365.pdf

75. www.reddit.com/r/BasicIncome/comments/2ioovd/kuwait_gave_almost_4000_to_every _citizen_in_2011

76. www.unicef-irc.org/publications/pdf/IWP_2016_21.pdf

77. wkms.org/post/senior-citizens-study-how-money-makes-better-brain-functioning#stream/0

78. www.nber.org/programs/ag/rrc/rrc2015/papers/3.3%20-%20Ayyagari,%20Frisvold.pdf

79. onlinelibrary.wiley.com/doi/10.1111/jcpp.12621/full

80. www.econ.ucla.edu/alleras/research/papers/MP%20final.pdf

81. www.sciencedirect.com/science/article/pii/S0305750X17301092

82. tntoday.utk.edu/2017/11/16/ut-releases-preliminary-findings-people-fund-evaluation/

83. www.reddit.com/r/BasicIncome/wiki/studies

84. thepod.cfccanada.ca/sites/thepod.cfccanada.ca/files/BICN%20-%20Basic%20income%20programs%20and%20pilots%20-%202014_1.pdf

85. sange.fi/kvsolidaarisuustyo/wp-content/uploads/Universal-Basic-Income-A-New-Tool-for-Development-Policy.pdf

86. docs.google.com/spreadsheets/d/1Y1ahKuNd8abBgLRU5jmqWi_ewC0HdH Z8rjDfx7LYiOc/edit#gid=0

87. www.nytimes.com/2013/06/14/opinion/krugman-sympathy-for-the-luddites.html?_r=0

88. twitter.com/NYTimesKrugman

89. www.adamsmith.org/blog/welfare-pensions/milton-friedman-on-the-negative-income-tax

90. bleedingheartlibertarians.com/2012/05/hayek-enemy-of-social-justice-and-friend-of-a-universal-basic-income/

reddit.com/r/BasicIncome/wiki/

91. digitalcollections.library.cmu.edu/awweb/awarchive?type=file&item=34315

92. www.basicincome.org/bien/pdf/2000BassoCostantin.pdf

93. www.bos.frb.org/economic/conf/conf30/conf30i.pdf

94. www.reddit.com/r/BasicIncome/comments/3rruew/during_the_nobel_prize _series_event_in_singapore/

95. www.basicincome.org/news/2016/02/international-christopher-pissarides-a-nobel-economist-argues-for-ubi-at-a-debate-in-davos/

96. www.youtube.com/watch?v=B1eOVU61mZE

97. twitter.com/umairh/status/366800162376519680

98. twitter.com/umairh

99. twitter.com/umairh/status/327845209226481664

100. twitter.com/umairh/status/334750695007875072

101. twitter.com/umairh/status/337910847743606787

102. twitter.com/erikbryn

103.
www.citizensincome.org/resources/Newsletter19993body.htm#Partnerships

104. www.skidelskyr.com/site/article/too-much-faith-in-markets-denies-us-the-good-life/

105. boilingfrogs.info/2012/11/08/guy-standing-precariat-angry/

106. www.youtube.com/watch?v=4WaA8zqjBSk

107. www.opendemocracy.net/ourkingdom/daniel-raventos-julie-wark/republican-call-for-basic-income

108.
www.economonitor.com/dolanecon/2014/01/03/the-economic-case-for-a-universal-basic-income/

109. www.zpub.com/notes/rfree10-b.html

110. www.egs.edu/library/john-stuart-mill/articles/principles-of-political-economy-abridged-with-critical-bibliographical-and-explanatory-notes-and-a-sketch-of-the-history-of-political-economy/book-ii-distribution/chapter-i-of-property/

111.
www.academia.edu/2698139/Two_arguments_for_Basic_Income_Thomas _Paine_1737-1809_and_Thomas_Spence_1750-1814_

reddit.com/r/BasicIncome/wiki/

112. blogs.lse.ac.uk/europpblog/2013/07/24/the-eurodividend-why-the-eu-should-introduce-a-basic-income-for-all-philippe-van-parijs/

113. www.scottsantens.com/yeah-but-who-is-going-to-pay-for-it-basic-income-alan-watts

114. www.altruists.org/static/files/Martin%20Luther%20King%20on%20
Citizen's%20 Dividend.htm

115. j.mp/MLK4BasicIncome

116. www.youtube.com/watch?v=gf3n-L5FDy0

117. www.youtube.com/watch?v=ImXjgdIVsWE

118. www.fljs.org/sites/www.fljs.org/files/publications/Murray.pdf

119. www.huffingtonpost.ca/hugh-segal/guaranteed-annual-income_b_3037347.html

120. transitionculture.org/2012/08/21/an-interview-with-charles-eisenstein-something-in-your-heart-knows-that-this-is-what-life-is-supposed-to-be-about/

121. www.youtube.com/watch?v=d5WRGvfw_70

122. www.thenation.com/article/186129/snowden-exile-exclusive-interview

123.
www.facebook.com/peterjosephofficial/posts/58370
2995000193

124. www.youtube.com/watch?v=fto7Bn7m6dg

125. binews.org/2014/10/united-states-five-time-presidential-candidate-ralph-nader-supports-a-basic-income

126. www.youtube.com/watch?v=-vnB16E36EQ

127. www.youtube.com/watch?v=sZFnE94ni9I

128. www.cma.ca/Assets/assets-library/document/en/about-us/gc2015/delegates-motions-en.pdf

129.
d3n8a8pro7vhmx.cloudfront.net/bicn/pages/151/atta
chments/original/
1439928444/
Ontario_physicians_letter_to_Hon___Eric_Hoskin
s_(FINAL_August_17_2015).pdf?1439928444

130. ubie.org/brief-history-basic-income-ideas/

131. binews.org/2013/02/opinion-the-one-minute-case-for-a-basic-income

132. goo.gl/e8rZzI

133.
www.fljs.org/sites/www.fljs.org/files/publications/M
urray.pdf

reddit.com/r/BasicIncome/wiki/

134. www.scottsantens.com/tanf-is-terrible

135.
basicincomenow.wordpress.com/2014/12/15/how-to-fund-a-universal-basic-income-in-the-usa/

136. jetpress.org/v24/walker.htm

137. www.robinhoodtax.org/how/everything-you-need-to-know

138.
www.academia.edu/5305083/The_Automated_Payment_Transaction_
APT_Tax

139.
www.salon.com/2013/11/22/end_the_1_percents_free_ride_how_taxing_
land _would_solve _americas_ biggest_problems/

140.
www.uvm.edu/giee/pubpdfs/Flomenhoft_2012_Exploring_the_Alaska_
Model.pdf

141. www.yesmagazine.org/issues/cities-are-now/in-alaska-everyone-gets-paid-thousands-in-oil-dividends-per-year/

142.
www.bien2012.de/sites/default/files/paper_170_en.pdf

143.
www.nytimes.com/2014/10/30/upshot/quantitative-easing-is-about-to-end-heres-what-it-did-in-seven-charts.html

144. www.usbig.net/papers/144-Sheahen-RefundableTaxCredit.pdf

145.
www.iser.essex.ac.uk/research/publications/working-papers/euromod/em17-14

146.
www.academia.edu/3278736/Report_for_Working_Group_on_Basic_
Income

147. www.scottsantens.com/yeah-but-who-is-going-to-pay-for-it-basic-income-alan-watts

148. www.usbig.net/papers/144-Sheahen-RefundableTaxCredit.pdf

149. funding-programs.idilogic.aidpage.com/

150. medium.com/basic-income/wouldnt-unconditional-basic-income-just-cause-massive-inflation-fe71d69f15e7

151.
en.wikipedia.org/wiki/Quantity_theory_of_money

152.
en.wikipedia.org/wiki/Alaska_Permanent_Fund

reddit.com/r/BasicIncome/wiki/

153. laborstats.alaska.gov/cpi/cpi.htm

154. www.bls.gov/cex/2012/combined/income.xls

155. www.reddit.com/r/BasicIncome/comments/1syjw1/what_would_you_do_ about _local_variations_in _the/

156. www.reddit.com/r/BasicIncome/comments/20wz6e/i_think_we_should_ have _one_thread_with _all_the/

157. www.economist.com/blogs/democracyinamerica/2013/11/government-guaranteed-basic-income

158. www.bbc.co.uk/news/business-25415501

159. www.nytimes.com/2013/11/17/magazine/switzerlands-proposal-to-pay-people-for-being-alive.html?_r=0&pagewanted=all

160. timharford.com/2013/11/a-universal-income-is-not-such-a-silly-idea/

161. www.usatoday.com/story/opinion/2013/10/10/swiss-referendum-minimum-income-column/2945657/

162. youtu.be/07F1b3uPoGs

163. www.washingtonpost.com/opinions/free-money-might-be-the-best-way-to-end-

poverty/2013/12/29/679c8344-5ec8-11e3-95c2-13623eb2b0e1_story.html

164. decorrespondent.nl/541/why-we-should-give-free-money-to-everyone/20798745-cb9fbb39

165. www.cnn.com/2014/04/14/opinion/wheeler-minimum-income/

166. www.pbs.org/newshour/making-sense/whats-welfare-initiative-uniting-liberals-conservatives/

167. www.huffingtonpost.com/carl-gibson/the-case-for-a-basic-guar_b_5311330.html

168. www.newsweek.com/how-fix-poverty-write-every-family-basic-income-check-291583

169. www.scientificamerican.com/article/how-to-prevent-the-end-of-economic-growth/

170. www.youtube.com/watch?v=xtpgkX588nM

171. www.youtube.com/watch?v=4WaA8zqjBSk

172. www.youtube.com/watch?v=c7nY0UWrSIA

173. www.youtube.com/watch?v=6pd-gBlKE8c

174. www.youtube.com/watch?v=ViywrpAyVdY

175. fivethirtyeight.com/features/universal-basic-income/

176. www.economonitor.com/dolanecon/2014/01/03/the-economic-case-for-a-universal-basic-income/

177.
www.economonitor.com/dolanecon/2014/01/13/coul
d-we-afford-a-universal-basic-income/

178.
www.economonitor.com/dolanecon/2014/01/27/a-
universal-basic-income-conservative-progressive-
and-libertarian-perspectives-part-3-of-a-series/

179.
www.pieria.co.uk/articles/creative_destruction_basi
c_income_and_the_
jobs _of_the_future

180. www.reddit.com/u/2noame

181. amzn.com/lm/RWMEMI9G196XT

182. www.basicincome.org/research/

183. www.reddit.com/r/BasicIncome/wiki/support

184. www.reddit.com/r/BasicIncome/wiki/support

185. www.meetup.com/BasicIncome/

186. www.reddit.com/r/BasicIncome/wiki/support

187. ubie.org/overview-established-facebook-
pages-basic-income

Made in the USA
Monee, IL
05 November 2026

67972638R00042